DON'T WASTE THE STORM

2nd Edition

Copyright © 2012, by Gerald and Christy Williams

ISBN   978-0-9857190-0-5

All rights reserved. Except for brief excerpts for review purposes, the reproduction or utilization of this work in whole or in part in any form by any electronic, mechanical or other means, now known or hereafter invented, including xerography, photocopying and recording, or in any information storage or retrieval system, is forbidden without the written permission of the authors.

Copies of this book are available at:
www.geraldandchristy.com

Printed in the United States of America.

COMING SOON

- *Will All the Righteous Ladies Please Stand Up!*

- *Consider Your Loaves*

- *The Christian Co-Ed*

- *Know Your Enemy: Satan*

All books will be available at **www.geraldandchristy.com**

DEDICATION

This book is dedicated to

*Christians past and present who battle (d)
Storms
for the cause of Christ;*

And to

*Our amazing and beautiful daughters;
Madison and Meagan;
You are our inspirations.*

DON'T WASTE THE STORM

2nd Edition

How to Have Joy & Peace in the Midst of Life's Trials

By:
Gerald and Christy Williams

TABLE OF CONTENTS

DON'T WASTE THE STROM 1
COMING SOON 3
DEDICATION 4
DON'T WASTE THE STORM 5
INTRODUCTION 9
STORM 12
THE DISCIPLES' WASTED STORM 13
LIFE LESSONS FROM THE DISCIPLES' WASTED STORM 17
    LESSON 1: GOD IS ALWAYS ON THE JOB. 17
    LESSON 2: DON'T WORRY. 19
    LESSON 3: GOD IS IN OUR STORMS WITH US. 22
    LESSON 4: WE MUST HAVE FAITH. 26
    LESSON 5: DON'T WASTE THE STORM, OR YOU WILL LIKELY REPEAT IT. 28
    SUMMARY OF THE DISCIPLES' WASTED STORM 30
GRATITUDE 31
PRAYER OF GRATITUDE 32
CATEGORIES OF STORMS 34
STAGES OF A STORM 35
PERSONAL STORMS 37
RESOLUTION 38
PERCEPTION OF THE STORMS 39
STORMS OF OLD 41
SECRET STORM 45
SEEKING HELP IN YOUR STORM 49
STORM WATCH/STORM WARNING 51
ROLE OF GOD IN OUR STORM 57
ROLE OF SATAN IN OUR STORM 73

WHEN YOU FEEL YOUR STORM IS TOO LONG! 80
   CONSIDER THE BLIND MAN 81
   CONSIDER THE WOMAN WITH THE ISSUE OF BLOOD 83
   THE WOMAN WITH THE ISSUE OF BLOOD: THE 12 YEAR STORM 85

STORM PROOF YOUR LIFE 90

STEPS TO SALVATION 93
   PLAN OF SALVATION 94

TESTIMONIALS 96

AUTHORS' TESTIMONIAL 100

AUTHORS' ACKNOWLEDGEMENT 104

ABOUT THE AUTHORS 106

JOIN THE DON'T WASTE THE STORM MOVEMENT 108

Present Storms and Future Glory

Romans 8:18

¹⁸ I consider that our present sufferings are not worth comparing with the glory that will be revealed in us.

Romans 8:28

²⁸ And we know that in all things God works for the good of those who love him, who have been called according to his purpose.

INTRODUCTION

Have you ever REALLY noticed how life works? We can be going through life making what we think are great decisions; treating the people we love well, trying to live a life that's pleasing to God, etc. When out of nowhere, one of life's many storms blows our way. Perhaps an un-expected financial crisis slams into our life. Or maybe the winds of infidelity blow into our marriage. Or perhaps the death of a love one shatters our foundation. Whatever the circumstance may be, it has the ability to bring us to our knees. We are dazed and confused and unsure how to proceed.

If we are honest, this is the time that many of us begin to make decisions based upon our emotions; often times resulting in making bad situations worse. Quite often, we also find ourselves angry…even with God.

Now, why is this? It is our contention that it is simply because we fail to recognize God in our storms. We fail to consider the possibility that God has allowed storms to come into our lives for specific times, for specific purposes, and for specific outcomes.

Our goal in writing this book is to give you a gift. The gift is learning to appreciate and to be thankful for the storms that assail your life. **Don't Waste the Storm** will hopefully be an aid in helping you to focus on the lessons IN the storm and NOT the storm itself.

It will assist you in going through your life's storms with patience, strength, stability, and even joy. *James 1:2-4 states: My brethren, count it all joy when you fall into various trials,* [2] *knowing that the testing of your faith produces patience.*[3] *But let patience have its perfect work, that you may be perfect and complete, lacking nothing.*[4]

Furthermore, we have included in **Don't Waste the Storm** several worksheets for you to complete. We have included these because we don't want you to just read through the material. We want to prompt you to work through your storms. We hope that these exercises give you new tools to use in dealing with future storms.

It is our sincere hope that **Don't Waste the Storm** blesses your Christian life and journey. Now, let's get started! By the way, we highly encourage you to read this book in conjunction with your bible. No book, including this one can replace God's word.

STORM

Definition: Any event or trial that causes discomfort, pain, or distress in a person's life.

Starting

Today: Trust,

Obey &

Rely on the

Master

THE DISCIPLES' WASTED STORM

Mark 4:35-41

(*Jesus teaches the disciples the proper way to handle life's storms.*)

That day when evening came, he said to his disciples, Let us go over to the other side. [35]

Leaving the crowd behind, they took him along, just as he was, in the boat. There were also other boats with him. [36]

A furious squall came up, and the waves broke over the boat, so that it was nearly swamped. [37]

Jesus was in the stern, sleeping on a cushion. The disciples woke him and said to him, "Teacher, don't you care if we drown?" [38]

He got up, rebuked the wind and said to the waves, "Quiet! Be still!" Then the wind died down and it was completely calm. [39]

He said to his disciples, "Why are you so afraid? Do you still have no faith?" [40]

They were terrified and asked each other, "Who is this? Even the wind and the waves obey him!" [41]

Background:

Jesus had recently healed a man's withered hand on the Sabbath day. He had also selected the 12 disciples, performed a few miracles in their presence, and had begun to teach multitudes through the use of parables. Now presently, Jesus and the twelve disciples board a boat to cross to the other side of the Sea of Galilee.

Day of the Storm:

The disciples have not yet fully comprehended all of who Jesus is and what he is capable of in their lives. That is why they will later exclaim *"Who is this? Even the wind and the waves obey him!"* That is also why they fail to take advantage of the storm that blows their way. They, in essence waste their storm.

> **The disciples wasted their storm.**
>
> **Wasted Storm-** a storm in which important life lessons sent by God are not learned.

LIFE LESSONS FROM THE DISCIPLES' WASTED STORM

Lesson 1: God Is Always On The Job.

While the waves were ferociously beating against the boat, Jesus lay asleep at the stern. What??? How in the world could Jesus sleep while the disciples were THINKING they were seconds from drowning?

Jesus could sleep because he knew WHO was in charge, even of nature itself. He was then and he still is today! Interestingly, Jesus was sleeping at the stern. As you may know, the stern is the place on a boat where the steering takes place.

When the storms of your life come (and oh yes, they most certainly will come) and beat upon your life boat; allow Jesus to guide you through your storms. He will NEVER steer you wrong. It may even seem at times that Jesus is disconnected from your problems or asleep on the job. But, he never truly is. Trust him to guide you through.

Lesson 2: Don't Worry.

The disciples spent a whole lot of time worrying about the storm. Can you not see them desperately trying to throw buckets of water out of the boat, only to have the waves refill the boat with water again and again? Can you imagine their frustration; their exhaustion; their panic and feeling of hopelessness?

Now, look at your life. Can you see yourself doing all that you can to fix whatever is broken in your life? Many sleepless nights, worrying, crying, searching for answers, but failing to remember what Jesus has said; failing to take Jesus at his word.

- *Philippians 4:6 says-Don't worry about anything. Instead, tell God about everything. Ask and pray. Give thanks to God.*

- The Hebrews writer adds in **Hebrews 13:5 -God has said, 'I will never leave you or abandon you'.**

- And, we must not forget the words of the wise man *I have been young, and now am old; yet have I never seen the righteous forsaken, nor his seed begging bread. (Proverbs 37:25)*

Although concern is normal, as true children of God we are instructed to never worry. Worrying will not solve our problems. It will just rob us of peace and joy in the midst of our storms.

When God is in control of our lives, no matter how strong, mighty, or ferocious our life storms may be there is no cause for worry. In fact, our worry is an insult to God. It tells him that we are not quite sure (despite all the previous storms that he has brought us through), that he is able.

> **There is never a true cause for worry.
> Our worry is an insult to God.**

Lesson 3: God Is in Our Storms with Us.

Jesus had already told the disciples that he would be with them and that they would make it to the other side. This is the implication of **"Let us go to the other side."** Their destination was known and certain, and Jesus had given them assurance that he would be with them all the way. What calm and peace should have filled their souls at the sound of those words!

> *Let us go to the other side.*
>
> *God has already promised us Heaven.*

He has guaranteed us safety and a Heavenly Home

Likewise, Jesus has already informed those of us who are true believers that we too have a destination; we too are going to the other side. Our destination is heaven. He has also given us assurance that he will be with us all the way.

Consider the following verses.

- *Mathew 28:20- "Teaching them to observe all things whatsoever I have commanded you: and, lo, I am with you always, even unto the end of the world."*

- *John 14:2, 3- "In my Father's house are many mansions: if it were not so, I would have told* you. I go to prepare a place for you. And if I go and prepare a place for you, I will come again, and receive you myself; that where I am, there you may be also."

- **Philippians 3:20-** But our citizenship is in heaven. And we eagerly await a Savior from there, the Lord Jesus Christ.

> **Revelations 21:4**
>
> He will wipe away every tear from their eyes, and death shall be no more, neither shall there be mourning, nor crying, nor pain anymore, for the former things have passed away.

So yes, storm clouds will continue to rise in our lives. But, God is in our storms with us. And, we will never shift off course, we will never get lost, shipwrecked, or drown as long as we allow God to direct our life boat. We must never lose sight of the fact that God is in our storm with us and has guaranteed us safety and a heavenly home.

Lesson 4: We Must Have Faith.

Mark 4:40: He said to his disciples, 'Why are you so afraid? Do you still have no faith?'

The simple truth is that the disciples did not have sufficient faith in Jesus. Jesus recognized this and needed the disciples to recognize it in themselves. If they had sufficient faith, they would not have needed to wake Jesus from his nap. They would have been content to ride out the storm, trusting that since Jesus brought them to it, he would bring them through it.

There is no way to over-emphasize the need for faith in our daily walk and in dealing with our storms. When our storms hit, Jesus asks us the same questions that he asked his disciples. Why are you so afraid? Do you still have no faith? It is easy to claim faith, but our actions show whether we HAVE faith. Just as with the disciples, God requires us to have a non-wavering faith in him. Without faith, we can never truly please him. And, without sufficient faith, we will always waste our storms!

> *For without Faith it is impossible to please him.*
> *Hebrews 11:6*

Lesson 5: Don't Waste the Storm, or You Will Likely Repeat It.

Believe it or not, life storms don't just appear on the horizons of our lives. They are sent our way for a purpose. They are designed to teach us, to stretch us, and to grow us in a way that will be beneficial to us, to God, and to others on our spiritual journey.

The key with storms is that we MUST learn the lessons that the storms are designed to teach. If we fail to learn the lessons, God may intervene and calm the storms anyway. But, it is very likely that he will send those storms back to our lives again and again in various ways in hopes that we will learn the lessons.

So, let us learn from every storm that we face. And, let us also learn not to waste them. It is interesting how the disciples later find themselves in yet another storm as they follow Christ. (You can read more about the second storm in our book, **Consider the Loaves**.)

> *A Wasted Storm will be a Repeated Storm.*
>
> Repeat. Repeat. Repeat. Repeat.

SUMMARY OF THE DISCIPLES' WASTED STORM

- Before the storm, make sure that God is at the stern of your life's boat.

- During the storm, don't worry. Instead: STOP, PRAY, & GIVE THANKS to God for what you do have. It is amazing how prayers of gratitude can change our perceptions of our storms.

- Ask God to guide you through the storm and reveal to you the lesson you are to learn.

- "Know" that God is in your storm with you and that he will never forsake you.

- Rejoice in the midst of the storm.

GRATITUDE

Gratitude unlocks blessings in our lives. It even unlocks the blessing of peace during our storms. And, every single person has reasons to be thankful. So what are yours?

List 5 things you are grateful for today.

1.
2.
3.
4.
5.

SUGGESTION

Start a gratitude journal. On a daily basis, write down 5 things throughout the day that you are grateful for. Your list may change daily. Also, the things on your list may be big or small. Learn to appreciate all of your blessings.

PRAYER OF GRATITUDE

If you are a parent, then you have probably had the experience of your child being exceptionally nice and helpful because he/she wanted something from you. Your child had an ulterior motive. You have probably also imagined how wonderful it would be if your child behaved that way without actually wanting something.

God, our father is no different. He loves it when we come to him just to give thanks; with no ulterior motives. Be honest with yourself. When was the last time that you've actually done that?

Below: Write a prayer of gratitude to God. Thank him for specific blessings in your life. In this prayer, do not ask God for anything. Just thank him; even for your present storm.

<u>PRAYER</u>

CATEGORIES OF STORMS

Are you currently experiencing any of these storms?

(No matter the storm, God is always bigger than the storm.)

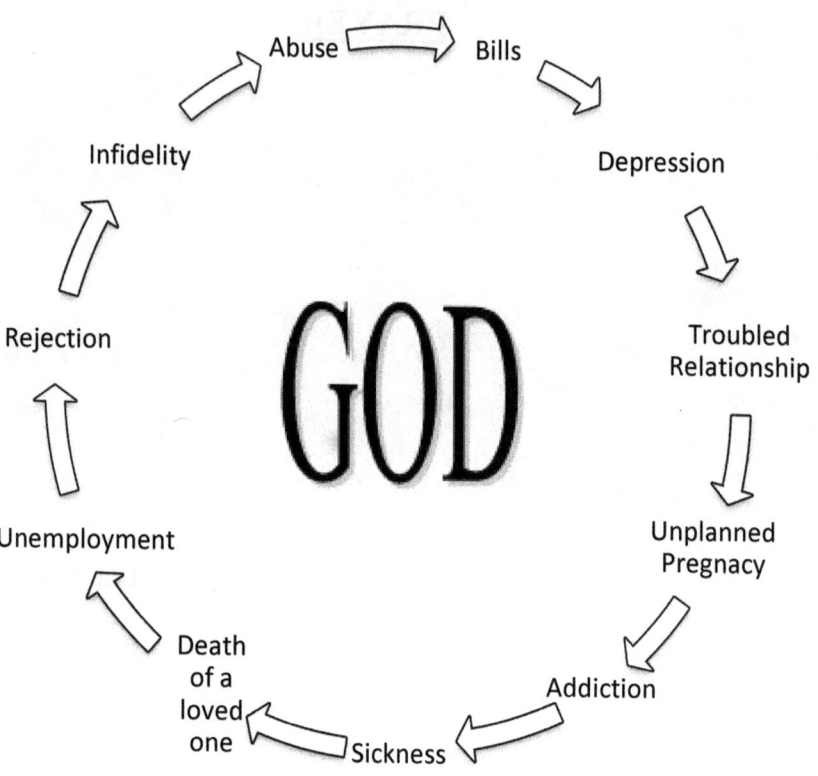

STAGES OF A STORM

Which stage of your storm are you in? Check one.

❏ **Entering a Storm:**

This is the stage where an event or trial, that causes us discomfort, pain, or distress enters our life. It is the stage where we can decide how we will deal with the storm. Will we waste it by complaining and getting angry with God and others? Or, will we decide to focus on the lessons in our storm? When we enter a storm, we need to Stop, Pray, and ask God to lead us through the storm.

❏ **In the Midst of a Storm:**

In this stage, we have been in our storm for a while (hours, days, months, years). But, we must not give up. We must keep our faith, and trust God. When it seems as if things are progressively getting worse; still trust God. We must trust him no matter what. Remember, he is looking for people who are willing to put their unwavering trust in him.

Why should we trust God? We should trust him because he has proven himself. He has brought us through many previous storms in our lives. He will not fail us now.

❑ Exiting a Storm:

This is the stage that we often long and pray for; relief from the storm. Congratulations! It is at this point that we have hopefully learned the lesson meant for us. We now have an additional life experience that can help someone else in his/her storm.

PERSONAL STORMS

1. List and explain 3 storms in your life that you wasted.

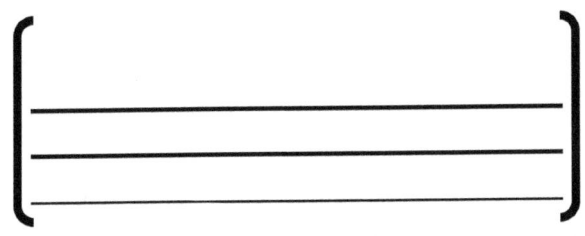

2. List and explain 3 storms in your life that you did not waste.

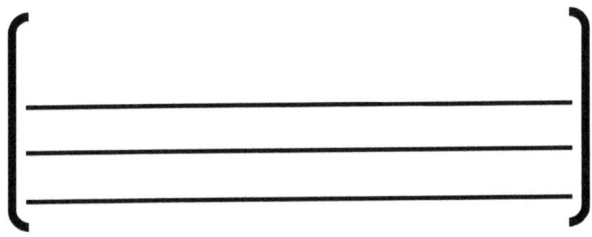

3. Specifically, how will you now deal differently with your storms?

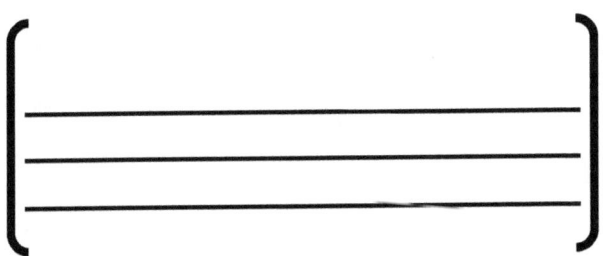

RESOLUTION

1. How would you like to see your current storm(s) resolved?

2. Are you able to embrace the fact that God may resolve your storm(s) in a way not desired by you? Why, or why not?

3. In what way can you let go of control of the storm and allow God to work it out for you?

PERCEPTION OF THE STORMS

The saying that perception is reality has a lot of truth to it. The way we choose to perceive our storms will have a profound impact on our storms and our lives. We must understand that choosing to bemoan our storms will not stop them from coming into our lives. And, it will not make them go away any sooner.

What bemoaning our storms will do is weaken our faith and our spirit and also lead to both physical and mental ailments. It often causes us to develop hypertension, migraines, nerve damage, etc. It also often causes us to become anxious and depressed.

However, if we choose instead to perceive our storms as blessings sent by God to enrich our lives and to perfect us, we can maintain joy and a peace that passes all understanding even in the midst of our storms. We can then take advantage of our storms and not waste them.

Remember: As a man thinks in his heart, so is he. (Proverbs 23:7) So, if you think your storm will defeat you; it will. And, if you know you will triumph over your storm; you will.

STORMS OF OLD

Don't waste your storm. It is the perfect time and condition for God to show up and reveal his power in your life. And once he does reveal his power in your life, your life can then become a testimony to others.

Daniel

Daniel was in a storm when he was cast into the lion's den. But God showed up and delivered Daniel by closing the mouths of the lions. And as a result, Daniel was elevated in status and the whole country worshipped God.

Job

Job was in the midst of a storm when Satan took everything from him but his very life. Yet, God showed up and blessed Job with much more at the end of his storm than he had to begin with. And, that's saying a lot considering at the beginning Job was already the richest man in his region.

Joseph

Joseph was in a storm when he was placed in a pit, sold into slavery and then later cast into prison. But God showed up and raised Joseph to a position of second in command to Pharaoh himself. He became the savior, not only of the Egyptians but for his own family as well. And, Joseph's salvation of his people secured the lineage that Jesus was to come through.

Sarah

Sarah was in a storm when she, after many years of marriage, was still unable to conceive a child. But God showed up in due time and Sarah, at the age of 90, was blessed with a son named Isaac. And, it was through Isaac's seed that all nations were blessed.

Jesus Christ

And our Lord Jesus was in a storm, with the fate of the human race in his hands while he hung on the cross. But God showed up and in three days he raised Jesus from the dead. And, now Jesus sits in heaven at the right hand of God.

You

So, what storm of life are YOU battling today? No matter what it is God can turn any storm into a testimony of victory. And, just as it was with Job, your ending too can be better than your beginning. Don't waste the storm.

> *Storms have been around for a long time. Everyone from Job, Sarah, to Jesus has experienced them. We will not be exempt.*

SECRET STORM

There are some storms in our lives that everyone knows about. We can't hide them. And then there is another category of storms; our *secret storms*.

These are the storms in our lives that we feel no one else knows about. We carry around the extra burden of always trying to keep them hidden in the closet. But, there are a few facts that we should know about our secret storms.

1. **Our secret storms are already known by God.**

    - ***Psalm 90:8** tells us: "Thou hast set our iniquities before thee, our **secret** sins in the light of thy countenance."*

    - Since our secret storms are already revealed to the one who can judge us; perhaps we should stop investing so much time and energy in trying to hide them from others.

    - Not all of our secret storms are sinful. Even for those non-sinful ones; we must not allow embarrassment or guilt to keep us from obtaining help.

2. Our "secret" storms are often NOT secret.

- Often, our secret storm is a "well-known" secret.

- There are usually those who already know about it.

- There are usually those who are already sharing it with others.

3. There are others who have gone through the same storms and are willing to help.

- It is encouraging and uplifting to talk to someone who has dealt with the same storm and has come out on the other side.

- We should be able to turn to someone for help when we are battling a secret storm.

- ***1 Corinthians 12:26*** *"And if one member suffers, all the members suffer with it; or if one member is honored, all the members rejoice with it."*

- Find those who are willing to share the burden of your storm with you. A shared burden is often a lightened burden.

SEEKING HELP IN YOUR STORM

There are some life storms that we can battle alone. There are others that we cannot. It is very important to know when to seek help for our storms. What a horrible feeling it is to feel alone and disconnected from everyone when we're battling our storms! It makes our storms just that much harder to bear.

Sometimes, help in our storms comes in the form of a listening ear of a friend. Other times, it comes from church leadership or clergy. There are also times when we need to seek help from professionals who have been trained to deal with our specific types of storms.

Suggestion:

1. Have a mental list of people with whom you feel comfortable confiding about your storms.

2. The next time you are feeling overwhelmed by a storm, reach out to one of those individuals on your list.

3. Recognize when you need to seek professional help in dealing with your storm.

STORM WATCH/STORM WARNING

Warning Signs

We have all been watching television and had our programming interrupted by an emergency weather alert. How did the weather person know bad weather was on the way? He/she knew because he/she had been watching the signs.

Now, if we think back on the past storms in our lives, many of them gave us warning signs before they hit. Sometimes, we chose to ignore the signs. At other times, we just didn't know what signs to look for.

The types of storms that give us warning can usually be minimized or avoided. That is why it is so important to pay attention to the warning signs.

Let us illustrate with storms that occur way too frequently and affect every demographic.

Storm 1: Domestic Violence

Most domestic violence perpetrators do not start off hitting their victims.

- The violence usually begins with verbal abuse /name calling. **(STORM WATCH)**

- It may then escalate to a periodic shove or push. **(STORM WATCH)**

- After a while, the violence escalates even more with a slap. **(IMPENDING STORM)**

- The violence finally reaches the level of a beat-down/hospitalization. **(STORM)**

But, there were warning signs all along the way.

Storm 2: Sickness

Sometimes, our sickness comes suddenly and without warning. Other times, there are warning signs along the way. And, if we pay attention to the warning signs, we can avoid the full fledge storm all together.

- You gain 30 pounds, and can no longer fit into any of your clothing. (STORM WATCH)

- You notice that after a period of time, you are out of breath just walking across a room. (STORM WATCH)

- You notice that you have begun to have chest pains. (IMPENDING STORM)

- You have a heart attack. (STORM)

Storm 3: Adultery

Marriage was designed by God to be a wonderful union between one man and one woman. But when couples fail to follow God's plan on how to maintain a great relationship, the storm of adultery can blow in.

- You start having a causal conversation at work with an attractive person of the opposite sex. (STORM WATCH)

- You start meeting after work with that person and soon realize that you really enjoy their company. (STORM WATCH)

🌀 You start telling the person about your marital problems. (STORM WATCH)

🌀 He/she hugs you and tells you that you deserve better. (IMPENDING STORM)

🌀 You wake up in someone else's bed and have committed adultery. (STORM)

SUMMARY

God loves and has use for each of us in his kingdom. But, think about how much more service we can give him if we are physically, mentally, and spiritually able. There are some storms in life that can be avoided. We have to learn to avoid those that we can!

Finally, let's take a moment and think about some of the past storms in our lives. We may have never experienced domestic violence, a heart attack, or adultery. But it is likely that we have all experienced some storms that came with warning signs. From this point on, we need to make sure that we are able to identify the warning signs in our lives.

Role of God in Our Storm

There are three that make up the godhead (Trinity). They are God the Father, God the Son, and God the Holy Spirit. They each play a distinct role in our storms. However, they agree as one and have one common objective. That objective is to transform us into more perfect spiritual beings.

In our Storms, God the Father is:

A. Sender of the storm

- (***Psalm 107:25***)- *For he commanded, and raised the stormy wind, which lifted up the waves thereof.*

B. Trier of our faith

- **(Psalm 66:10)**- *For thou, O God, has proved us, thou has tried us, as silver is tried. The Lord tries the righteous…*

C. Deliverer from the storm

- **(Psalm 34:19)**- *Many are the afflictions of the righteous: but the Lord delivered him out of all of them.*

- **(Psalm 107:28-30)**- *Then they cry unto the Lord in their trouble, and he brings them out of their distresses.* **He makes the storm calm***, so that the waves thereof are still. Then are they glad because they are quiet;* **so he brings them unto their desired haven.**

Discussion

What you may not know and what a closer reading of Psalm 107: 25-30 reveals is that God will both bring storms into our lives as well as deliver us from those same storms. The storm that God delivered his people from in verses 28-30 was actually sent by him in verse 25.

Why did God do this? And, what is the meaning of this for our lives today? The reason God did this then and the reason he still does this today is so that he can try our faith. And once our faith is tried, God will make us perfect, established, strengthened, and settled. (1 Peter 5:10)

BUT, notice the state of the people before God stepped in and calmed the storm; before he guided them to their desired haven. Psalm 107: 26 says that their souls melted because of trouble. Then, verse 27 states: ***"They reel to and fro, and stagger like a drunken man, And are at their wits' end."***

Sometimes, our storms will bring us to our wits' end. But, God will never put more on us than we can bear. He is ever watchful and, when the time is right, he will also bring US to our desired haven.

In our Storms, **God the Son/Jesus Christ** is:

A. Shelter

- *(Isaiah 25:4)- For thou has been a strength to the poor, a strength to the needy in his distress, **a refuge from the storm**, a shadow from the heat, when the blast of the terrible ones is as a storm against the wall.*

- *(Isaiah 32:2)- And a man shall be as a hiding place from the wind, and as a covert from the tempest.*

- Isaiah prophesied that a man (Jesus Christ) would come into the world and be a shelter/ hiding place from storms. And, that man, Jesus Christ is still our storm shelter today. When the storms of life assail us, we are assured that if we turn to him, he will give our soul protection in the midst of our storm.

B. Mediator

- *(1 Timothy 2:5)- For there is one God, and one mediator between God and men, the man Christ Jesus.*

C. Intercessor

- *(Romans 8:3)- It is Christ that died, yea rather, that is risen again, who is even at the right hand of God, who also makes intercession for us.*

D. Advocate

- *(1 John 2:1)-* *We have an advocate with the Father, Jesus Christ the righteous.*

E. Rest

- *(Mathew 11:28)-* *Come unto me, all ye that labor and are heavy laden, and I will give you rest.*

- *(Hebrews 2:18)-* *For in that he himself hath suffered being tempted, he is able to succor them that are tempted.*

Discussion

In his roles as intercessor, mediator, advocate, and rest, Christ provides much for us while we are going through our storms. (That is why we should not react in the same way to storms as those who are without Christ.) He hears our cries for help and then goes to God our Father on our behalf.

He serves as a go-between. And, he is there to take our loads upon himself. That is why the scripture tells us to cast all our cares upon him, for he cares for us. (1 Peter 5:7)

And, Jesus Christ is uniquely qualified to advocate for us in a way that no one else is. For *Hebrews 4:15, 16 says: We have not a high priest which cannot be touched with the feeling of our infirmities, but was in all points tempted like as we are, yet without sin. Therefore, let us come boldly unto the throne of grace that we may obtain mercy, and find grace **to help in the time of need.***

So, no matter how ferocious the storms may be that we encounter, we are well equipped not only to endure the storms but to overcome them. We overcome them through Christ Jesus. And when we do, we grow stronger in our faith.

In our Storms, **The Holy Spirit** is:

    A. Comforter

- (**John 15:26**)- *But when the Comforter is come, whom I will send unto you from the Father, even the Spirit of truth, which proceeded from the Father, he shall testify of me.*

The Holy Spirit can comfort us throughout our life storms. For, it can give us joy and peace even in the midst of our storms. Just as we turn to our loved ones for comfort and peace; we can, with even more assurance turn to the Holy Spirit.

So, how exactly does the Holy Spirit comforts us? It comforts us through the divine word of God. Therefore, the next time that you are facing a life storm, pick up the word of God and allow it to sooth your spirit. It can comfort you like no one else can.

However, the Holy Spirit does not and will not force its comfort upon us. It will not force itself into our lives. It will only provide comfort to us if we allow our spirit to align with its spirit. (Galatians 5:25)

B. Guide

- *(John 16:13)- Howbeit when he, the Spirit of truth, is come, he will **guide** you into all truth: for he shall not speak of himself; but, whatsoever he shall hear, that shall he speak: and he will show you things to come.*

- *(1 Corinthians 2: 10-12)-*

    But God hath revealed them unto us by his Spirit: for the Spirit searches all things, yea the deep things of God.

    For what man knows the things of man, save the spirit of man which is in him? Even so the things of God know no man, but the Spirit of God.

    Now we have received, not the spirit of the world, but the spirit which is of God; that we might know the things that are freely given to us of God.

C. Teacher/Instructor

- *(1 Corinthians 2:13)- Which things also we speak, not in the words which man's wisdom teaches, but which the **Holy Ghost teaches** comparing spiritual things with spiritual.*

D. Intercessor

- *(Romans 8:26)- Likewise the Spirit also helps our infirmities: for we know not what we should pray for as we ought: but **the Spirit itself makes intercession** for us with groanings which cannot be uttered.*

- *(Romans 8:27)*- *And he that searches the hearts know what is the mind of the Spirit, because he makes intercessions for the saints according to the will of God.*

> **HOLY SPIRIT**
> *GUIDE*
> *COMFORTER*
> *INTERCESSOR*
> *TEACHER/INSTRUCTOR*

Discussion

Don't you just love the roles of the Holy Spirit in our lives! When we are going through a storm and are without even the right words to say to God; the Holy Spirit steps in to our rescue.

The Holy Spirit helps us in our time of trouble and weakness. (This should also remind us that we are never truly alone in our storms.) It intercedes for us with groanings that cannot be uttered. It also asks for things on our behalf, according to the will of God.

This is important because oftentimes when we pray, we pray amiss. Oftentimes we pray to be delivered from a storm when that is not in our best interest. Sometimes we may even pray for certain solutions from the storm which are not in our best interest.

The Holy Spirit knows what is and is not in our best interest and is able to intercede for us according to the will of God.

Furthermore, notice whom the Holy Spirit will intercede for. It does not intercede for everyone. It only intercedes for the saints of God. What a special privilege to be saints of God when we are going through our storms! With the aid of the Holy Spirit, we should be encouraged not to waste our storms.

ROLE OF SATAN IN OUR STORM

Text: The Book of Job, Job 2:1-6, 1 Peter 5:8-10

Job 2:1-6

Again there was a day when the sons of God came to present themselves before the Lord, and Satan came also among them to present himself before the Lord. [1]

And the Lord said to Satan, "From where do you come?" So Satan answered the Lord and said, "From going to and fro on the earth, and from walking back and forth on it." [2]

Then the Lord said to Satan, *"Have you considered* **My servant Job***, that there is none like him on the earth, a blameless and upright man, one who fears*

God and shuns evil? **And still he holds fast to his integrity, although you incited Me against him, to destroy him without cause."**[3]

So Satan answered the Lord and said, "Skin for skin! Yes, all that a man has he will give for his life." [4]

"But, stretch out Your hand now, and touch his bone and his flesh, and he will surely curse You to Your face!"[5]

And the Lord said to Satan, behold he is in your hand, but spare his life."[6]

1 Peter 5:8-10

Be sober; be vigilant; because your adversary the devil walks about like a roaring lion, seeking whom he may devour. [8]

Resist him, steadfast in the faith, knowing that the same sufferings are experienced by your brotherhood in the world. [9]

But may the God of all grace, who called us to His eternal glory by Christ Jesus, after you have suffered a while, perfect, establish, strengthen, and settle you. [10]

Discussion

Job 2:1-6 relays the story of the second time that Satan approached God in regards to Job. In Job 1, Satan went before God and informed God that he had been going to and fro in the earth and walking up and down in it. God then asked Satan had he considered Job because Job was such a righteous man.

Satan responded that the reason Job could be so righteous was because God had placed a hedge around him and blessed him in every way. He contended that if those things were taken away, Job would curse God to his face. So, God gave Satan permission to do whatever he wanted to Job except take his life.

Satan then got very busy. He sent several storms in Job's life. He took from Job all of his material blessings (his oxen, donkeys, sheep, and camels). He also killed all of Job's 10 children. Though Job mourned, the bible says that in all of this Job sinned not, nor did he charge God foolishly.

That is where Job Chapter 2 picks up. Satan has once again presented himself before God. And, once again God asks Satan has he considered Job. God also points out to Satan that although Satan incited God against Job without cause, Job still maintained his integrity.

Satan now contends that the only reason Job has done so is because Satan has not been allowed to touch

Job's body; his health. Satan adds that he is sure that if he is allowed to do so, Job will curse God to his face. Once again, God grants Satan permission to send storms into Job's life. He again gives Satan permission to do anything to Job that he wants except take his life.

The entire book of Job allows us to see a man of God dealing with storm after storm that is sent his way. And, they are major life storms. He deals with the loss of his family, his health, his wealth, and his relationships.

So, what role does Satan play in our storms? Satan is there solely for the purpose of trying to use our storms to turn us away from God.

As 1 Peter 5:8-10 points out Satan is still walking about on this earth as a roaring lion, seeking whom he may devour. He is entreating us (just as he did Job) that in the midst of our storms, we should charge God foolishly. We should curse God and die.

But, we must strive to be like Job. Even in the midst of our storms, we must hold on to our integrity. We must give God the honor and praise that is due him. We must not allow Satan to use our storms to turn us against our God.

WHEN YOU FEEL YOUR STORM IS TOO LONG!

Have you been in your storm longer than YOU think is necessary? Do you feel that you have learned all that you need to learn from your storm and that now it is time for God to come and rescue you? If so, you are not alone.

So often, we get caught up in thinking that our storms are just about us. And once we feel we've gotten the message, we no longer see a reason for the storm to continue. However, our storms are not just about us. Sometimes our storms linger to aid others and oftentimes to show God's glory.

Consider the Blind Man

(John 9:1-3)

As he went along, he saw a man blind from birth. [1]

His disciples asked him, "Rabbi, who sinned, this man or his parents, that he was born blind?" [2]

"Neither this man nor his parents sinned," said Jesus, "but this happened so that the works of God might be displayed in him." [3]

This blind man's storm began with his birth. For, he was born blind. And, it lasted for many, many years. He wasn't actually healed of his blindness until he was an adult.

But Jesus makes the point to the disciples that the blind man's storm wasn't just about him.

- It was sent in his life so that the works of God could be shown in him.

- It was sent so that others could benefit from the knowledge of the amazing power of our God.

So the next time you are in a storm that seems to be lasting too long, you can take comfort in the knowledge that God is most likely working something big in your life. He is preparing to show his glory, not only to you but to others on your life's path.

Consider the Woman with the Issue of Blood

(Mark 5:25-34)

And a woman was there who had been subject to bleeding **for twelve years.** [25]

She had suffered a great deal under the care of many doctors and had spent all she had, yet instead of getting better she grew worse. [26]

When she heard about Jesus, she came up behind him in the crowd and touched his cloak [27]

Because she thought, "If I just touch his clothes, I will be healed." [28]

Immediately her bleeding stopped and she felt in her body that she was freed from her suffering. [29]

At once Jesus realized that power had gone out from him. He turned around in the crowd and asked, "Who touched my clothes?"[30]

"You see the people crowding against you," his disciples answered, "and yet you can ask, 'Who touched me?'"[31]

But Jesus kept looking around to see who had done it.[32]

Then the woman, knowing what had happened to her, came and fell at his feet and, trembling with fear, told him the whole truth.[33]

He said to her, "Daughter, your faith has healed you. **Go in peace and be freed from your suffering.**"[34]

The Woman with the Issue of Blood: The 12 Year Storm

Talk about a storm that has seemed to go on too long! There are few who would argue with the fact that this woman had been in her storm for a long time.

Here is what we know.

- She bled every single day, 24 hours a day, for 12 years.

- Over twelve years, she went from doctor to doctor.

- Not only did the doctors not heal her, her bleeding became worse.

- She spent ALL her money seeking help for her bleeding condition.

- She was in multiple storms: a health storm, a financial storm, and an emotional storm.

Discussion

Can you relate to having to deal with a long lasting storm? Have you ever been forced to deal with multiple storms at the same time? If you've experienced either of these, then you know firsthand the toll that these types of storms can take on our faith, our peace, and our hope.

However, the woman with an issue of blood serves as a reminder to us of the importance of holding on to our faith and our hope in the midst of our storms. Even when we begin to feel that all hope is gone, we must trust that God will never abandon us. We must trust that he is able to deliver us from our storms. It is only by holding on and confidently looking to him for deliverance will we activate the power of faith.

Sometimes, we underestimate the power of faith. The power of faith brings us through our storms. The power of faith can even change our storms. It tells God in the words of Job "Though he slays me, yet will I trust him." This type of faith can be developed and increased through continuous study and meditation on God's word.

However, we must not put God on a timetable. His timing is simply not our timing. But be assured, he has not forgotten or forsaken us! And when the time is right, he will deliver us from our storms. Can't you hear him saying, similarly to what he said to this woman, "Son/Daughter …go in peace and be freed from your suffering (storm)."

Don't Waste the Storm
PLEDGE

> Pledge– I will not Waste another Storm!

After reading *Don't Waste the Storm*, I understand that storms are inevitable and are sent into my life for a reason. From this point forward, when I encounter one of life's storms I will:

- First pray for strength and for understanding.
- Find scripture about my storm.
- Give thanks to God for my blessings.
- Keep my hope and faith.
- Be concerned but not worried.
- Be joyful and at peace throughout my storm.

I_____, have read and fully understand how to not waste a storm. I will instead have joy and peace in the midst of life's trials.

STORM PROOF YOUR LIFE

In real life, smart people don't wait until a storm comes before they build a storm shelter. None of us can stop the rain, tornadoes, and hurricanes of life. We just have to be prepared when they come.

Even though we don't have control over our life storms; there are ways to storm proof our lives. Jesus tells us how in Mathew 7:24-27.

Mathew 7:24-27

Therefore whoever hears these sayings of mine and does them, I will liken him to a wise man who built his house on the rock[24]

And the rains descended, the floods came, and the winds blew and beat on that house; and it did not fall, for it was founded on the rock.[25]

But everyone who hears these sayings of mine, and does not do them, will be like a foolish man who built his house on the sand: [26]

And the rains descended, the floods came, and the winds blew and beat on that house; and it fell. And great was that fall.[27]

If we want to have a storm proof life, we must HEAR Jesus and DO what he has commanded. And then, we must be like the wise man. Our lives must be built on the solid rock. That is the only way we can obtain salvation and a storm proof life. Has your life been storm proofed?

STEPS TO SALVATION

(Isaiah 59:1, 2)

Surely the arm of the LORD is not too short to save, nor his ear too dull to hear.[1]

But your iniquities have separated you from your God; your sins have hidden his face from you, so that he will not hear.[2]

(Romans 3:23)- *For all have sinned, and come short of the glory of God.*

Salvation Premise:

In order for us to have confidence and assurance during life's storms, we must be in a committed relationship with God. Thankfully, God through his word has provided the way for us to enter into a divine relationship with him. Below is God's biblical plan of salvation.

PLAN OF SALVATION

- **Hear.**
  - ❖ Romans 10:17- *"So then faith cometh by hearing, and hearing by the word of God."*
- **Believe.**
  - ❖ John 8:24- *"I said therefore unto you, that ye shall die in your sins, for if you believe not that I am he, you shall die in your sins."*
- **Repent** of your sins.
  - ❖ Luke 13:3, 5- *"I tell you, Nay: but, except you repent, you shall all likewise perish."*
- **Confess.**
  - ❖ Mathew 10:32, 33 - *"Whosoever therefore shall confess me before men, him will I confess also before my Father which is in heaven. But whosoever shall deny me before men, him will I also deny before my Father which is in heaven."*
- **Be Baptized**.
  - ❖ Mark 16:16- *"He that believeth and is baptized shall be saved; but he that believeth not shall be damned."*

- **Remain faithful** unto death.
  - ❖ Revelations 2:10- *"...be thou faithful unto death, and I will give thee a crown of life."*

Discussion

Once we have grasped hold of salvation, there is no reason why we should not have joy and peace in the midst of our life's storms. For, we understand that we have a God who will bring us TO our storms, comfort us IN our storms, and take us THROUGH our storms.

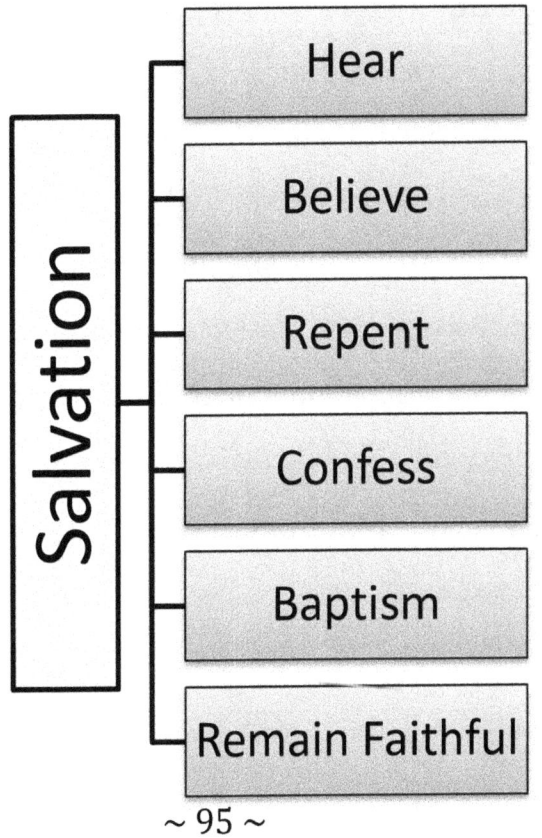

TESTIMONIALS

THE STORM: *I never waited on God to send the right husband to me. Nor did I seek his guidance in choosing a mate. As a result, I found myself married 3 different times to 3 unfaithful men who were not godly. They were not faithful to God and they were not faithful to our marriage vows.*

WASTED & NOT WASTED: *I obviously wasted the first storms. However, I did not waste the last one. After the 3rd marriage, I understood that God was chastising me for not looking for men who were godly, and for not waiting on him. Now that I am patiently waiting on God to choose my mate, my life has been great. I would also like to add that even in those storms, I feel that God still blessed me with my kids.............* **Ms. Carey**

TESTIMONIALS CONTINUED.....

THE STORM: *It was my first year coaching high school football. During the off season, I decided to go hunting with another coach and a few friends. It was then that the accident happened. Someone fired a shot at a deer. But, instead of shooting the deer, he accidentally shot me in the leg. My leg was shattered. And, after making it to the hospital, the doctors had to amputate my leg above the knee.*

NOT WASTED: *The nurses would always cover my face while changing my bandages. On day 4 of being in the hospital, I told the nurse to let me see my stump as she changed the bandage. When I saw it, I SCREAMED and the nurse nearly fainted. But, I was just joking with her! Now, I talk to other people and to kids who have lost limbs and reassure them that life afterwards can still be great........* **Coach Mason**

TESTIMONIALS CONTINUED.....

THE STORM: *I watched my best friend die in my arms after a car accident. I am a young man and I cried like a baby. I continued to ask God why? My sister told me that God might have been trying to get my attention because I was living too fast.*

STORM WASTED: *I heard her. But, it is 3 years later and to be honest, I am still drinking, smoking, and living that same lifestyle. Don't get me wrong, I think about my friend all the time and I visit his grave whenever I get a chance............***Chris Smith**

TESTIMONIALS CONTINUED…..

THE STORM: I was struggling to pay my bills. Every day I received calls from bill collectors with threatening messages. I starting feeling depressed and felt like the walls were closing in on me.

NOT WASTED: When the collectors started calling, I decided to start sharing scripture with them about how God was working my situation out. Their whole tone changed. They were not as hostile as before………**Kelvin Masey**

All testimonials are real. However, names have been changed to protect privacy.

AUTHORS' TESTIMONIAL

Like many of you, we have gone through our fair share of storms. But we would like to share one in particular with you. We remember it like it was yesterday. It was November 4, 2008. It was the day many of us in the U.S. know as Election Day. Like everyone else, we could feel the excitement in the air. This would be a monumental and historical election, however it was decided. At the end of the night, we would have either our first African American president or our first female vice president. As an attorney and political science minor, I think I was even more excited than most.

I had already planned out my day. I was going to go to my Dr.'s appointment for my monthly checkup (I was 4 ½ months pregnant) and then I was going to camp out in front of the television set all day and night long. I wasn't going to miss a minute of the action.

At the doctor's, everything proceeded as usual. All the tests were normal. When the appointment was almost over, the doctor said "Let's just listen to that baby for a minute and then you can get out of here." It was then that our world turned upside down. After minutes of trying unsuccessfully to find a heartbeat, our doctor called in another professional. It was after the second doctor couldn't find it either that our doctor became concerned. Her teasing about a difficult baby stopped and she made me an immediate appointment at another center.

From there, the storm worsened. At the end of the day, I had been sent to 4 different places for numerous tests and meetings with medical professionals. (These meetings and tests would continue for months.) I was told everything from there was a likely possibility of death for me, to it was almost impossible for my baby to make it. A normal heart rate for a baby is 60-120, and my baby's heart rate was barely registering 12.

I could say that we had no doubts or fears, but that wouldn't be true. However, we had learned some powerful lessons over the years in dealing with previous storms. So, as soon as I made it home, we went to our knees in prayer. We prayed with 100% confidence that God could change things. We didn't know if he would, but we knew that he could. After that, we opened up the Word and received comfort. Then, later on that night, as originally planned, we watched the election results come in and witnessed the selection of the new president elect.

Over the next months, we were repeatedly sent to a perinatologist in another state. We would use quite a bit of the three hour ride to pray to God. Over time however, we found that our prayers were changing. Our initial prayers were for God to fix the situation and to heal our bodies. (Looking back, we clearly see that in our prayers we were attempting to bend God's will to our own.) Later however, our prayers were for the Lord to give us the strength to accept his will, whatever it may be. It was at that point of ultimate and complete surrender that our lives changed. It was then that we felt we had truly learned the lesson in the storm.

At our last perinatologist appointment, the Dr. stated that he did not think he would need to make any further appointments for us. He said that everything that was initially looking wrong had reversed itself. And, although every now and then he could see the baby's heart rate drop, he felt that it was due solely to the baby being ultra-sensitive to the medical instruments being used during examinations.

Well, our normal doctor wasn't quite so optimistic. So, on the day of delivery, there were special doctors and nurses in the delivery room-just in case there was trouble. However, we delivered a very healthy and beautiful baby girl. All of her tests, (as well as mine) came out well and we were allowed to go home two days after delivery. Today, she is an extremely smart, active and most importantly healthy little girl.

The Lesson: **S**tarting **T**oday: Trust, **O**bey, & **R**ely on the **M**aster. God doesn't really need our help in the storms of life. He just needs us to trust him unconditionally. For, when we are weak, then we are made strong. His power is made perfect in our weakness.

Gerald and Christy Williams

AUTHORS' ACKNOWLEDGEMENT

First, we would like to thank and acknowledge God for all of the experiences and life storms he has sent our way. Although we have not always enjoyed them in the moment, they have undoubtedly been and continue to be the catalyst for intense growth and development in our lives. We hope that at the end of our life journeys, we too can say like Job that we have been tried and have come out as gold.

Next, we would like to thank each and every one who has played a role in our spiritual growth and development. We thank you for your encouragement, guidance, advice and prayers. We would also like to thank all of those who have supported us along the way.

Last, but not least, we would like to give special thanks to all the readers of **Don't Waste the Storm.** This book was written especially with you in mind. We hope that you take comfort in the knowledge that you are not alone in your storms. And, when the next storm blows your way, we have confidence that you are now equipped with the tools to not waste it.

God Bless.

Gerald and Christy Williams

ABOUT THE AUTHORS

Gerald and Christy Williams are a married writing team who collectively has over 35 years of experience in ministry. They love to write about their greatest passion: God and his love for mankind.

Gerald uses his experiences as an educator, youth minister, and deacon and Christy uses hers as an attorney and bible teacher to write about issues that are prevalent in today's society. It is their desire that each of their books instills hope, and help individuals to form closer and more meaningful relationships with God.

Gerald is also an active motivational speaker. He has spent over 10 years speaking to diverse groups. He has a special love however for speaking to teen groups and young adults.

Gerald and Christy can be contacted at:

geraldmw@hotmail.com

&

www.geraldandchristy.com

Join the Don't Waste the Storm Movement by:

1) Telling someone how this book has helped you.

2) Posting a short video on youtube.com about one of your storm experiences.

3) Purchasing a *Don't Waste the Storm* book for a friend who is experiencing one of life's storms.

Visit www.geraldandchristy.com for more details

www.ingramcontent.com/pod-product-compliance
Lightning Source LLC
Chambersburg PA
CBHW070248100426
42743CB00011B/2175